THE ULTIMATE CONVERSATION

IS THAT YOU, GOD?

ALSO WRITTEN BY
RUTH HOVSEPIAN

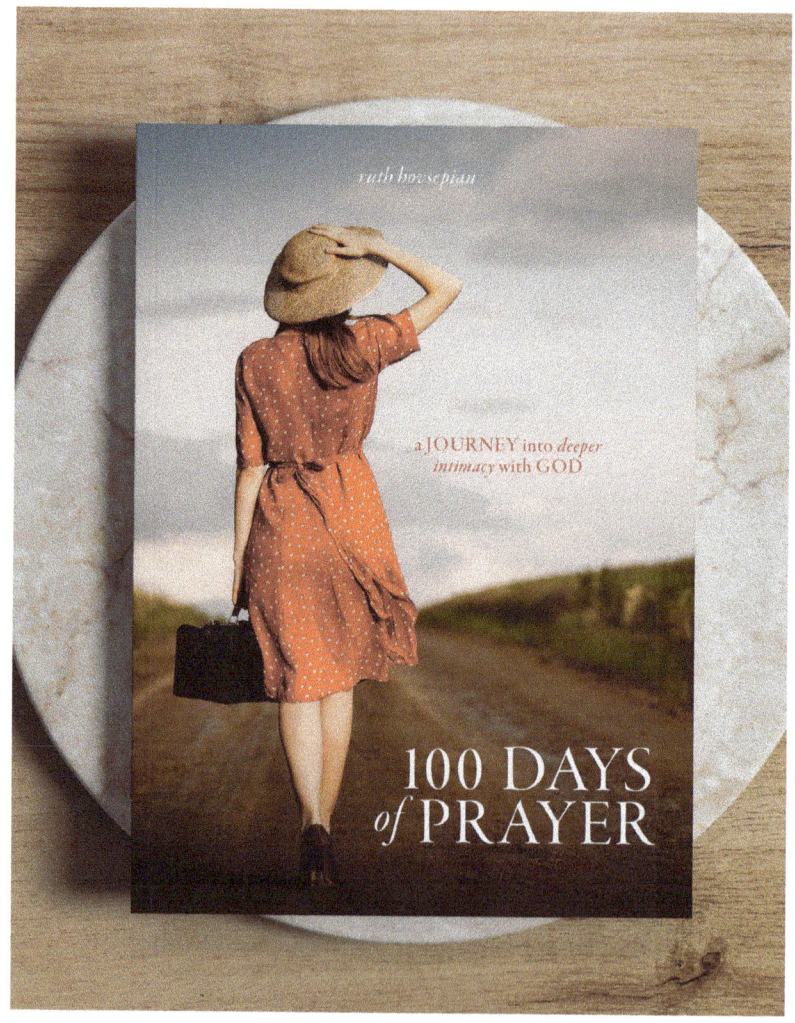

100 DAYS OF PRAYER:
A journey into deeper intimacy with GOD

BIBLE STUDY

THE ULTIMATE CONVERSATION

IS THAT YOU, GOD?

RUTH HOVSEPIAN

Edited by Ann-Margret Hovsepian
Graphic design by Alexis Livingston

ISBN: 978-1-962581-40-0

THIS BOOK BELONGS TO

_____

_____

CONTENTS

PRAY

P

**Praise Him and recognize Him
for who He is. Our Father.**

*Our Father in heaven,
hallowed be your name.
– Matthew 6:9*

R

**Repent of sin in your life.
Rejoice in Christ's forgiveness.**

*And forgive us our debts, as we also
have forgiven our debtors.
– Matthew 6:12*

A

**Ask God for help for yourself
and others. Help to meet physical needs,
for wisdom, healing, and deliverance.**

*Give us today our daily bread. And lead us not
into temptation, but deliver us from the evil one.
– Matthew 6:11 & 13*

Y

Yield to God in humble submission.

*Your kingdom come, your will be done,
on earth as it is in heaven.
– Matthew 6:10*

A NOTE FROM

RUTH

Are you ready to study and learn more about prayer and grow your prayer life? So many of us have lost our passion for prayer or don't consider it to be an essential part of our Christian life.

Some would like to pray but don't because they lack confidence or know how to pray.

Prayer is work. Prayer is purposeful. Prayer is powerful.

Even with this knowledge, we often do not pray because we find it easier to attempt and fix situations ourselves than to take the time to pray and wait for God's response.

I don't know what made you pick up this book, but I believe the Lord is calling you to prayer. My desire is for you to recognize God's voice as you move through this Bible study and let Him work in your heart.

You may have many different feelings about prayer, and some may even be conflicting. As you go through this Bible study, pray and consider God's invitation to you to spend this extraordinary time with Him.

Together we will examine answers to these questions: What is prayer? Does prayer work? What are some obstacles to prayer? and more.

Something fundamental inside the human spirit cries out and prays to a higher being, GOD. But there is something way more special in this. God is inviting YOU to prayer with Him. It's a PERSONAL invitation of love and faithfulness to HIS will. He wants you to find that with Him.

As you go through the sessions, you will need your Bible. You will also be invited to respond to some thought-provoking questions to answer as they apply to your personal life. This Bible study will challenge you with what you believe prayer means to you. Work through each session as far as you like. Go at your own pace. There is no time limit to the study.

Let this study ignite your passion for prayer again if you have fallen away from prayer. Let it breathe new life into a possible dead prayer practice. Join Him in this personal, intimate place called prayer.

Let's take this personal journey into deeper intimacy with GOD together as we discover PRAYER.

Ruth Hovsepian

"Is anyone among you in trouble? Let them pray.
Is anyone happy? Let them sing songs of praise."

JAMES 5:13

In Search of Answers

"Is anyone among you in trouble? Let them pray. Is anyone happy? Let them sing songs of praise." (James 5:13)

I struggled with prayer most of my life. I wanted to build a relationship and be nearer to God. I would hear others talk about their prayer lives and how they heard God's voice and their walk with Him. But when it was time for me to pray, there was an awkwardness. I never knew what to say. What words to use. How to express my thoughts.

The fact is that God was a stranger to me. I had heard about Him from birth. I had accepted Jesus in my life at twelve, but I had never formed a personal relationship with Him yet. I've come to realize there are many individuals like me. They also want to have an intimate relationship with God, but they struggle with prayer.

It is helpful to think of your early attempts at prayer as a conversation you would have with someone you just met. Naturally, you will feel awkward—you don't know God yet. Not yet in a deep and personal way.

You must take the time to push through the initial awkwardness and meet with God regularly. Only time and practice allow you to develop a more intimate relationship. An enduring relationship that is deep and will maintain you through life's storms. A relationship that comforts you during life's darkest moments and reminds you are not alone and that you have a friend who will never leave you. Getting to this point in your relationship with God will take time and intentional effort.

Here are some fundamental points you should reflect on as you develop and strengthen your prayer life.

What Prayer Is

Prayer is a conversation between you and God.

This statement sounds straightforward on the surface. But when you first start praying, it can feel like a monologue. After all, you are the one doing all the talking while still waiting for responses. Or are you?

It's easy to overlook God's voice (reply) because He doesn't always respond instantly or in the way we expected. You might pray about money worries only to find twenty dollars a day or two later when you are out walking. At that moment, you may have forgotten about your prayer.

Perhaps you pray about a family member's impending surgery and fail to consider her speedy recovery. These are answered prayers. You simply aren't aware of them.

Start your talks, your prayer time, with God by asking Him to open your eyes to see how He works in your life and the lives of those around you. Ask that the Holy Spirit remind you and make you aware of all the answered prayers around you.

I find it helpful to use a prayer list, recording who and what I am praying for. Create a list for yourself; make sure to add the date to your prayers. Later, you'll be able to look back and see how God has answered every request you've made.

Every Prayer Is Answered

You can't presume your prayer is unanswered if God does not give you what you have prayed about. God answers His children's prayers. Every prayer is answered. Your prayers may be answered differently than you want or in your timeline.

You may pray that a child's illness is cured. God may answer your prayer only after your child has been ill for five, ten, or even twenty years.

This is where struggling with prayer comes in. Doubts will distract you. You may ask, "What is the point of prayer if I don't get what I want when I want it?"

God Is Not a Vending Machine

It is disheartening, but some Christians believe that praying to God is like using a vending machine. You put in the correct amount, select the item you want, and, voila, the vending machine spits out the thing you paid for. Christians believe that if you say the correct words at the right time, then poof, God will grant your desire!

The problem with this way of thinking is that prayer is about forming a relationship with the great Creator of Heaven and Earth. The One who knit every one of your cells together and knows you more deeply than you know yourself (Psalm 139:13–14).

In a healthy relationship, you have the freedom to say "yes" or "no" to someone's request. You can say "yes" if you want to cook dinner this evening or "no" if you want to go out for dinner.

You have the gift of free choice. Yet many Christians can't understand how this same freedom should be applied within their relationship with God. They believe God's every answer to their prayers should be an instant and automatic "yes."

When you are always expecting God to do what you want, when you want, and how you want, you're not seeking a relationship with Him. You're seeking a transaction. This way of thinking is treacherous and creates space for disappointment and disillusionment.

God's Will Prevails

Accepting God's will can be challenging, especially when praying for something you believe heeds His will and is based on Scripture. You know you are not coming to God with your request as you would approach a vending machine. You understand the reality that God maintains the free will to say "no" to your request.

You may ask God to mend your relationship with your spouse or deliver your child from addiction. Maybe you are begging Him to heal your sister from a devasting illness.

Years or even decades may pass without God replying "yes" to your prayer request. God may have many reasons for denying you what you are asking for.

It could be to grow your faith, as He did with Joseph. At the end of more than a decade of hardship, Joseph was able to proclaim confidently, *"As for you, you meant evil against me, but God meant it for good, to bring it about that many people should be kept alive, as they are today"* (Genesis 50:20).

It could also be that God has already said "yes," but His timing is different than yours. Elizabeth, John the Baptist's mother, longed to have a child. But it wasn't until she was much older that God blessed her with her wish.

The delay had nothing to do with Elizabeth or her wish and everything to do with the timing of her request. God intended to use John the Baptist to go before the Messiah (Luke 1:17).

Regardless of how God answers your prayers, you can rest confident in one thing. God will always do what's best for you, as in Romans 8:28.

"And we know that for those who love God all things work together for good, for those who are called according to his purpose."

Why Pray?

At this point, you may be thinking, why should you pray when God will do what He knows is best and work everything out for your good? There's no real point in the conversation.

In Isaiah 38:1–8, Hezekiah had become deathly sick when the prophet Isaiah came to him and told him that the Lord was telling him it was time to set his affairs in order.

"Then Hezekiah turned his face to the wall and prayed to the Lord, and said 'Please, O Lord, remember how I have walked before you in faithfulness and with a whole heart, and have done what is good in your sight.' And Hezekiah wept bitterly." (Isaiah 38:2–3)

Then the Lord sends another message to Hezekiah. This time he is told God has heard his weeping, and fifteen years have been added to his life.

The story of Hezekiah and his prayer proves that prayers can sway God. God may have a specific plan, but your prayers may persuade Him to choose a different one.

No one can know the mind of God. It's simply too vast to contemplate. But repeatedly, the Scripture shows that God can and does adjust His plan based on the requests of His beloved children (that means you!)

Prayer Is a Conversation

A conversation is a way to share. Perhaps you share with your spouse how your day went. Or share with a friend an argument you had with a co-worker or an amusing anecdote that took place at school.

Prayer is a conversation. Start your prayer with sharing. Share with God about your day. Share with Him the good and bad. Ask Him for your needs. Ask for wisdom to deal with a situation. Or perhaps you need strength to continue to deal with a family member who is ill.

When you start to pray, it may feel as though God is not listening to you. There may be a great silence that you are tempted to believe God has turned a deaf ear or forgotten you.

Are you not silent when listening to someone speaking to you? Do you not wait until the person has finished what they have to say?

Your silence does not mean that you are ignoring the other person or have forgotten them. Your silence is only a show of your respect while listening to them speak.

It is the same with God. What you think as His silence is God patiently leaning in to hear your words. He is delighted to hear your voice and loves to listen to you speak.

God Is Not a Passive Listener

As your prayer life develops and matures, you will witness how God responds to your requests. David writes about God's answers to his cries in Psalm 18.

"In my distress I called upon the Lord; to my God I cried for help. From his temple he heard my voice, and my cry to him reached his ears." (Psalm 18:6)

David writes about how his prayers and cries reached God's ears. And then goes on to talk about God's response, *"...he was angry. Smoke went up from his nostrils, and devouring fire from his mouth; glowing coals flamed forth from him"* (Psalm 18:7b–8). God was furious on David's behalf.

It's easy to think that God is passively listening to your prayers and not doing anything about your requests. Yet Psalm 18 is a fantastic reminder that God is anything but passive. He is a God of action.

Be rest assured that when you pray, your prayers are not dismissed. God listens to every word you speak, and He will act on your behalf.

When Prayer Becomes Difficult

There will be days when your heart is too broken to pray. When life has knocked you down, you think you will never rise again. What do you do on those days? When words escape you.

During these times, it is good to remember Romans 8:26, which says, *"Likewise the Spirit helps us in our weakness. For we do not know what to pray for as we ought, but the Spirit himself intercedes for us with groanings too deep for words."*

When the pain is deep, and the waves of anguish continue to batter your heart, know this: the Holy Spirit that lives within you as a child of God is interceding on your behalf. The Holy Spirit is praying for you.

The Holy Spirit, at this moment, is communing with the Father, sharing your sharpest pain and deepest longings. He knows exactly what you need even when you are silent and pleads on your behalf.

I have found that during those dark times when words escape me, I repeat the name of God. Like a child who cries for their Father, repeating His name repeatedly.

In scripture, we read about the beggar or sick who called out to Jesus from the side of the road. Each time the needy and weak called out, Jesus stopped.

He stopped whatever He was doing and listened to those who needed Him the most. He was never too busy to hear and heal.

Pray Boldly

When you pray to God, do so boldly. Come into His presence with confidence. Enter His throne room, knowing that you are His beloved child—approach God as an heir.

Paul instructed the children of God in Hebrews 4:16, *"Let us then with confidence draw near to the throne of grace, that we may receive mercy and find grace to help in time of need."*

Not only must you approach confidently, but your prayers should be filled with confidence. Phillip Brooks said, "Pray the largest prayers. You cannot think a prayer so large that God, in answering it, will not wish you had made it larger. Pray not for crutches but for wings."

Prayer is a conversation. A deep and intimate conversation with God has the power to change you, change the situation you are in, and even change the world. But more importantly—more than the results or changes you see—it's the beginning of a deep and lasting relationship with the God who created you. That is worth everything.

Take your time as you reflect on these questions.
Have you ever considered prayer as an invitation to a conversation with God?

What are you searching for or hoping to learn from a study on prayer?

PERSONAL REFLECTION

If you have lost your excitement for prayer, list the reasons why.

What do you ask God for the most?

What is your confidence level in prayer?

How often do you make time for prayer?

"Let us then with confidence draw near to the throne of grace, that we may receive mercy and find grace to help in time of need."

HEBREWS 4:16

What is Prayer?

Ask several people what prayer is, and you will get all sorts of answers to this question.

I will give you several definitions to start off because prayer is not just one thing. Remember that prayer can be one or all of these and much more.

- Prayer is simply talking with God. It is an act, not an attitude. It can involve praise and adoration, thanksgiving, petition, repentance, and intercession.

- Prayer aligns your heart, will, and emotions with God's heart.

- Prayer is about an enduring, continuing, growing love relationship with God. To pray is to love.

WARNING!
DANGER!
PRAYER AHEAD!

Are you ready to take a chance? Because prayer is risky!

To pray is to change. God provides a path for you to take where through prayer your life can be filled with love. Love is freely given with no strings. With this love, we are changed.

Prayer Is the Foundation of Your Spiritual Life

When building a house, the first and most crucial step is to put in a solid foundation. Our lives can be compared to a structure (1 Peter 2:4–5). The foundation of our lives is as critical as it is for any physical building.

When your life is built on a solid foundation, dealing with stress, anxiety, problems, and struggles, you will quickly realize how firm and sure your foundation is–or isn't (Matthew 7:24–27).

Here are some foundational principles of prayer.

People all over the world pray. Nearly everyone has said a prayer, from the very influential to the child, at one point in their lives.

Even though nearly everyone prays, prayer is one of the most misunderstood practices in a Christian's life.

What is your understanding of what prayer is?

If you are like most people, including me, you have questions about prayer. If you are new to your faith in Christ, you probably have even more questions than most, and that is okay!

People from all walks of life question prayer and want to learn how to get started praying. Many believers want to pray but may need help understanding what prayer is and the priority of prayer in their lives.

People practice prayer with different motives. Many because they believe prayer works, and then some do not think that prayer works.

No matter how new you are to your faith and prayer, even the simplest of mumblings is a prayer.

Let me share a story about Alex.

Alex was new to his faith and had some reservations about prayer; he wasn't sure he would see results if he asked God for something. A situation came up in his life one day: He needed to pay his car insurance. Alex didn't have the full amount that he needed to pay. He began to get stressed about his situation but was afraid to ask God to help him with the money he needed.

He was in college and had a lot of other debts, and his work hours had been cut. The due date for his payment was getting closer and closer, and his stress was getting higher and higher. He needed $587 to pay for his car insurance in three days' time.

Alex told his friend John about his situation, and he encouraged Alex to pray about it. John half-jokingly said, "You never know. God could just put the money in your account."

Alex was so disheartened, he muttered, "I wish that would happen, but that stuff never happens to me." His friend prayed for him, and then Alex asked God with these simple words, "Could you just do it, God?"

The following day, as Alex was getting ready for school, he checked his bank account as he did daily. He knew he didn't have the money in it, but he checked anyway. To his utter astonishment, the account showed a deposit of $600. Alex did not know how or why. But it was there.

He couldn't believe that money was sitting in his account. When he called his friend and told him about the money, his friend couldn't believe the money had appeared just as it was needed. They both knew God had answered their prayers.

From that day forward, Alex acknowledged that God heard his prayers, and he didn't have to be afraid. His short prayer was enough.

Sometimes we are afraid or too discouraged to pray. We think we may not get the answer we are hoping for or that we won't get an answer right away, and we get discouraged.

Have you ever been discouraged and not been able to pray?

What did you do when you were discouraged? Did you give up?

Do you believe in the power of prayer?

You may struggle with prayer because you don't understand the principles of prayer and the purpose of praying. Let's dig into this together.

If we want to understand how to pray, how prayer works, why prayer works, and more, we need to get a good understanding of the foundation of prayer from the one who created it, God.

The Beginnings of Prayer

Prayer began in the Garden of Eden.

The first prayer in the Bible is seen in Genesis 3. It is the conversation between Adam and Eve when they hid from their Creator after "they heard the sound of the Lord God walking in the garden in the cool of the day" (verse 8). This is the first recorded dialogue in the scriptures between God and man. It is essential, therefore, to see dialogue as a necessary part of prayer.

Prayer is a conversation with God. There are two people represented in true prayer: you and God—and no one else. Others may be present, as in this account where there were two people and God, but prayer is always a conversation directly between a single human being and God himself. There are many kinds of prayer— intercession, thanksgiving, supplication, and various forms of petition—but fundamental to them is a conversation, an exchange between a man and God.

Read and write out Genesis 3:8-10.

That is the beginning of prayer. These verses deliberately depict an everyday scene in Adam and Eve's lives. It is interesting to note that the first prayer recorded in Scripture is only after the fall of man. Yet the account suggests that Adam and Eve had been continually delighted with the daily encounters and conversations with God. This seems to be a habitual act on God's part. He comes into the garden in the cool of the day to converse with the two that had come from his creative hand, and together they talked in the garden.

We are not certain how God appeared to Adam and Eve. God's appearance is not portrayed in Genesis, but He appeared as another human being. The remarkable thing is that in some faint way at least, this foreshadows that image of when God himself would come down and be a man—not just appear as a man but live as one of us—and all the prompting that has been conveyed in terms of prayer since the manifestation of Jesus our Lord. But in the Garden of Eden, God appeared as a man because Adam and Eve heard him walking in the garden. The sound of his footsteps alerted Adam and Eve that the time had come for their daily conversation and interaction with God.

What we see through this account is that the daily "prayer" Adam and Eve had with God up until this day had been was simple, casual, and uninhibited conversation.

Suddenly Adam and Eve had fallen, and sin had entered. The guilty duo hid, painfully aware of their nakedness, feeling ashamed and guilty. The narrative suggests that this is something foreign and unknown, that the opposite of this behavior was true before the introduction of evil. They would come with joy and readiness to greet their beloved Creator as He came into the garden to talk with them. That indicates what you find in prayer throughout the rest of Scripture, especially what Jesus taught us about prayer. We are not coming to a solemn, severe judge; we are coming to a loving Father.

When sin entered this paradise, the loving relationship Adam and Eve had with God broke; it was replaced with fear, guilt, and a reluctance to come before his presence. God did not walk away from them. Instead, He wanted to solve the problem and began asking Adam and Eve questions.

This scene is vital because a chasm appeared between man and God when man sinned, and God took the first step to bridge the chasm. That chasm separates us from God in our prayer lives. It can be caused by our fear or laziness to come before Him. What encourages me about this interaction in the Garden of Eden is that God took responsibility for changing what happened. His questions began a "prayer" between man and Himself.

These three questions from God are the start of the first prayer:

"Where are you?" (Genesis 3:9b)

"Who told you that you were naked?" (Genesis 3:11a)

"What is this that you have done?" (Genesis 3:13a)

Remember that God asks these questions not because he does not know their answers. He knows the answer to every question before he ever asks it. God never asks a question for his own benefit; no account of Scripture ever records a divine question that was asked to benefit the curiosity of God. Jesus was always asking his disciples questions, not because he did not know the answers, but because the questions would prompt an examination, a search on the individual's part, and that person would learn something from that search.

What is preventing you from approaching the throne of God in prayer?

What can you do to change your conversation with God?

How to Connect with Heaven through Prayer

Let's look at the following verses for a clearer picture of the connection between man and heaven through prayer.

"Let us then with confidence draw near to the throne of grace, that we may receive mercy and find grace to help in time of need." (Hebrews 4:16)

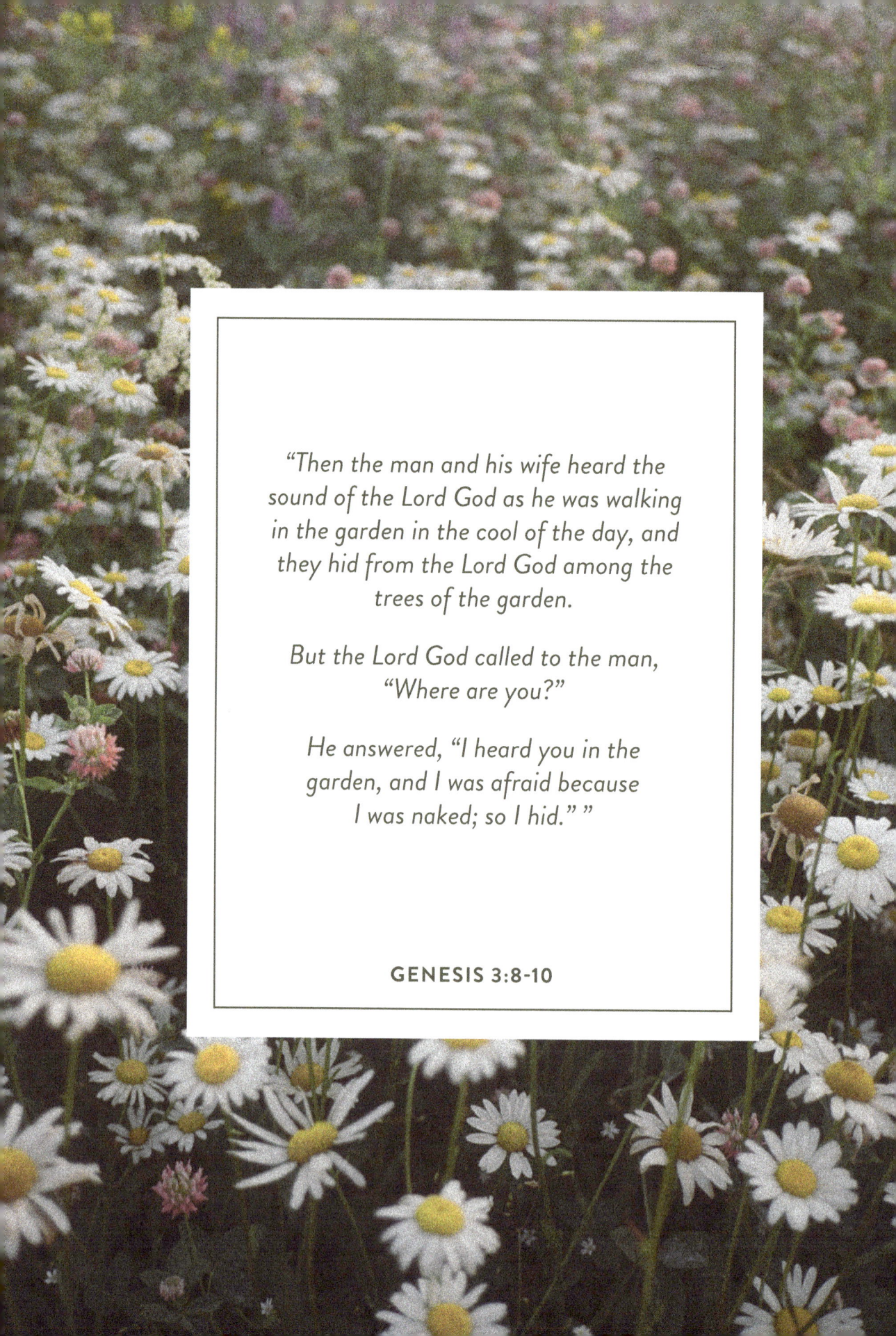

"Then the man and his wife heard the sound of the Lord God as he was walking in the garden in the cool of the day, and they hid from the Lord God among the trees of the garden.

But the Lord God called to the man, "Where are you?"

He answered, "I heard you in the garden, and I was afraid because I was naked; so I hid." "

GENESIS 3:8-10

"If my people who are called by my name humble themselves, and pray and seek my face and turn from their wicked ways, then I will hear from heaven and will forgive their sin and heal their land." (2 Chronicles 7:14)

"Rejoice always, pray without ceasing, give thanks in all circumstances; for this is the will of God in Christ Jesus for you." (1 Thessalonians 5:16–18)

"Truly, I say to you, whatever you bind on earth shall be bound in heaven, and whatever you loose on earth shall be loosed in heaven. Again I say to you, if two of you agree on earth about anything they ask, it will be done for them by my Father in heaven. For where two or three are gathered in my name, there am I among them." (Matthew 18:18–20)

"And he told them a parable to the effect that they ought always to pray and not lose heart." (Luke 18:1)

These verses show man's authority in prayer and how that authority determines God's will on earth.

But why must we exercise this authority? Why is this so important to prayer on earth? You may ask, "If God is sovereign, why do I need to pray?"

Let's look at that. You pray because...

MAN WAS CREATED TO HAVE DOMINION OVER THE EARTH.

John Wesley, a renowned theologian, said, "God does nothing but in answer to prayer."

Prayer is your invitation to co-labor with heaven, to ask God to be involved with the affairs of men on earth. This invitation from God to man will change the matters men are involved with.

God gave us authority over the earth. We must take that God-given authority and determine what happens here by praying.

Prayer is an invitation to discover and walk in your power, authority, and rights on earth.

Prayer is a way to position yourself as a faith channel for what heaven wants to influence on earth and in your circumstances.

You are a purposeful part of the plan of God in prayer.

When you fully understand this, you will not be discouraged in prayer, feel unworthy in prayer, or be intimidated.

Prayer is not just you saying words, but it is you working, praying, and speaking in cooperation with heaven!

Read and write out Deuteronomy 32:6.

God made you. You are dependent on God. We cannot show God to the world without accompanying our declaration with prayer.

Read and write out John 4:16.

Remember this truth: God created us to carry out His purpose on earth. God's purpose is our reason for existence; we are to do God's will. We are His voice, hands, and image on earth.

In what ways will you carry out His will on earth?

God never planned to rule the earth by Himself. Wow! Let that sink in. We are to work with Him.

This relationship with God that you have in prayer is one that you are encouraged to take soberly. You have been invited to the table with God through your prayer time. You have more power than you realize in declaring His will on earth, your family, and life situations.

God rules the unseen realm, mankind rules the visible realm on earth, and we enjoy communion with God through our spiritual life. Prayer is a beautiful fellowship with God that no other creature has been given.

So, to answer the question, "why do we need to pray?" Because...

PRAYER IS YOU CO-WORKING WITH GOD TO BRING HIS WILL TO PASS ON EARTH.

Read and write out 2 Corinthians 6:1.

Remember when I said that prayer has many different meanings? Here are several more:

- Prayer is an expression of man's relationship with the loving God and our participation in God's purpose for the earthly realm.
- Prayer is a process through which we learn to trust God.
- Prayer applies your whole self to God.
- Prayer is a spiritual communication between you and God, a way to become one with God and one with His will and His purpose on earth.

H.D. Bollinger said, "Prayer is being expressing relationship with another being."

Your prayers are how spiritual gain is made on earth. It's how you attain victory in the world. This foundation and understanding of prayer are essential for your healing, deliverance, patience, authority, freedom, confidence, assurance, peace, and boldness as a way of life.

One final definition...

- Prayer is essentially calling forth the will of God from the spiritual realm.

"True prayer is a way of life, not just for use in cases of emergency. Make it a habit, and when the need arises you will be in practice."

– BILLY GRAHAM

Why Is Prayer Important?

So far, we have looked at what prayer is in several different ways. Now let's learn why prayer is so important in the life of the Christian believer.

The answer to why prayer is so important comes from a question that some ask: "Why do we need to ask God to do anything when God has already determined He will do His will and purpose?"

The answer is twofold. First, God is faithful to Himself and His Word.

You have learned that God will not violate His Word and will not interfere with whoever has dominion on earth unless asked.

Second, it's how God gets His will accomplished on earth through mankind. It's crucial because what He wants to be done, He can't get it done without you praying! You and I have dominion over the earth.

Why is prayer important to you?

WHAT PRAYER IS NOT

I want to share with you what prayer is not. It is NOT. . .

- An attention-seeking activity (Matthew 6:5).
- A way to force God to do something you want.
- Vain repetition in your speaking (Matthew 6:7).
- A form of witchcraft or control of people or circumstances.

WHAT PRAYER IS

Prayer is a heartfelt, genuine conversation you, the believer, have with God. You don't attract attention to yourself. It's not repeating the same words or praying to get God to do something you want.

It's praying His will for what He wants to happen on earth.

Prayer is beautiful, incredible, and an amazing discipline in the life of a believer, and you get to be a part of that.

Read and write out 1 Thessalonians 5:16–18.

According to this verse above, the Bible says that we are to "pray without ceasing." This means having our minds always on the things of God and being in constant communication with him so that every moment may be as fruitful as possible.

This means that all through the day, you can whisper things to God; you can give Him praise, thanksgiving, adoration, and more. You can have times of repentance, intercession, or petition throughout your day.

"Without ceasing" can mean that your day is always filled with God and speaking to God at any time. He longs to hear from you and to have a conversation about anything in your heart.

Do you have a regular time each day that you read the Bible, pray, and are with God?

Are you easily distracted in prayer and turn to other things? How can you avoid this?

When you can see what something is NOT, you can see more clearly what it IS. Let's look at some reasons that confirm the importance of prayer.

Prayer Is a Direct Line of Communication

Talking to God through prayer is a direct line of communication between you and Him. You can talk to God and be assured that He hears you. You don't have to go through a priest, rabbi, or pastor. You can speak to Him yourself with great confidence. God is available at all times. Unfortunately, most believer's only use this line of communication when there is an emergency.

Read and write out 1 John 5:14.

Prayer Grows Faith

Your faith is strengthened when you pray. When you pray and see answers come to fruition, you are encouraged. Your faith is strengthened when you pray what seems like an impossible prayer and God answers it.

Your faith increases when that person you were praying for who needs a miracle receives it because you prayed. Your faith soars when you allow God to use you as a vessel of change for someone else.

If you have faith in God's Word, He will take the impossible and make it possible. Faith is simply taking God at His Word.

Allow God to use you.

"This is the confidence we have in approaching God: that if we ask anything according to his will, he hears us."

1 JOHN 5:14

Prayer Teaches Perseverance

Praying is vital to your Christian walk because it teaches you to persevere in troubling circumstances or seasons. You learn in times of trouble to be patient and wait. You may wait for an answer to your prayer for weeks, months, or years or never see the answer in your lifetime. Even though this can be tough, you will grow your faith and patience while waiting.

"Faith does the impossible because it lets God undertake for us, and nothing is impossible for God... Prayer throws faith on God and God on the world. Only God can move mountains, but faith and prayer move God." – E. M. Bounds

What are you praying for and waiting for God to answer?

Prayer Teaches Dependence on God

Total dependency is a rare quality in people. We don't want to rely on others. When you are determined to be a person of prayer, you learn to depend on God alone for answers. You recognize that you can trust Him and Him alone.

We believe in the power of prayer. Yet when it comes right down to it, when we face our own problems and trials, we often struggle to believe that God will hear us and answer. Unbelief and independence trap us. Our lack of faith and our fear of stepping out in dependence on Him get in the way. The truth is that our actions for God should be outside of our abilities.

Our actions should prove that we depend on Him and trust in His supernatural power to do the unattainable.

What trial are you facing today?

Will you put it all in His hands and step in to your faith that He will take care of it?

Prayer Is Powerful

There is power and strength in prayer, and we have yet to realize the full extent of it. We hesitate to ask. Miracles happen if we approach God in faith and prayer and ask Him to work in our lives, governments, and nations.

God's answers are powerful when we exercise our authority in prayer. The Church has not yet realized the strength and power behind prayer.

Well-known prayer author and intercessor, E. M. Bounds, wrote about the power of prayer:

"Prayer is power and strength, a power and strength that influences God, and is most salutary, widespread, and marvelous in its gracious benefits to

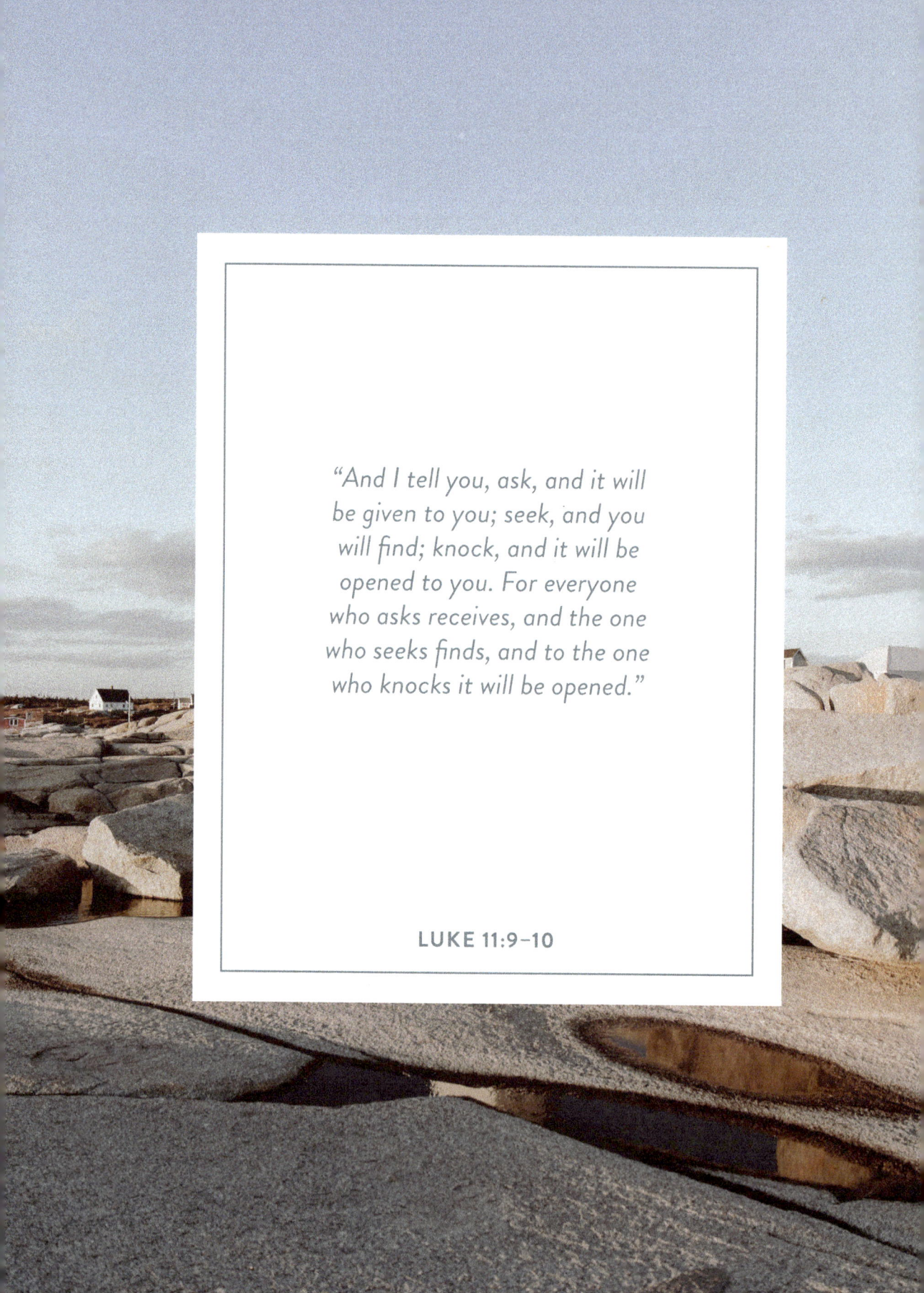

"And I tell you, ask, and it will be given to you; seek, and you will find; knock, and it will be opened to you. For everyone who asks receives, and the one who seeks finds, and to the one who knocks it will be opened."

LUKE 11:9–10

man. Prayer influences God. The ability of God to do for man is the measure of the possibility of prayer."

Prayer Grows Our Relationship with God

Prayer is connecting with God and telling Him all that is on our hearts and minds. Of course, He already knows it, but communication grows and develops a relationship. We should not pray only when we want or need something; He isn't our fairy godmother. Psalm 62:8 (NIV) says "pour out your hearts to him" because that level of personal conversation makes our relationship more intimate.

The more you trust Him, the more you will tell Him. And the more time you spend with Him in prayer and His Word, the more you will get to know Him and trust Him. Prayer should be the most intimate conversation we have with another. And God allows us to share that intimacy with Him through prayer.

Through prayer, you have a deeper fellowship with God. As you pray, you delight in Him, and He in you. There will be times when you long for fellowship with Him, and nothing else will satisfy you.

What other ways is prayer essential to you?

Prayer Builds Confidence

"And this is the confidence that we have toward him, that if we ask anything according to His will, he hears us. And if we know that he hears us in whatever we ask, we know that we have the requests that we have asked of him." (1 John 5:14–15)

This is powerful because as your confidence grows, you know God heard you, and when you know He heard you, you have the requests you prayed for.

God wants you to have so much confidence that you won't hesitate to ask Him. When you and I don't ask God for His will, this keeps us from what God would want to give us.

"You desire and do not have, so you murder. You covet and cannot obtain, so you fight and quarrel. You do not have, because you do not ask." (James 4:2)

"And I tell you, ask, and it will be given to you; seek, and you will find; knock, and it will be opened to you. For everyone who asks receives, and the one who seeks finds, and to the one who knocks it will be opened." (Luke 11:9–10)

Name something that you are NOT asking God for.

"The great tragedy of life is not unanswered prayer, but un-offered prayer."

— F.B. MEYER
(THE SECRET OF GUIDANCE)

"But when you pray, go into your room, close the door and pray to your Father, who is unseen. Then your Father, who sees what is done in secret, will reward you."

MATTHEW 6:6

How to Pray

"The prayer of a righteous man is powerful and effective." (James 5:16 NIV)

We have looked at a few good working definitions of prayer and some reasons it's important to pray, but how do we do it? Is there a particular way to pray? Are there any special mechanics? Do you pray prayers someone else wrote?

We will look at some biblical ways of praying and then some creative ways to pray.

If you ask, "How do you pray?" you will get as many different answers as there are people you ask. Some may tell you that they are not sure how to pray. Some may give you specific words and phrases to say. Some may even say it doesn't matter because "God hears you no matter what you say."

As you walk your Christian journey, you can't assume that everybody knows how to pray.

Prayer is the Christian believer talking to God. But prayer is not just about talking to God. That is one way of praying. It's also about communion with the one true God. Before we begin...

What does communion with God mean to you?

When you ask someone how they learned to pray, some say they learned in Sunday school class. Others may tell you that their mother taught them how to pray at night before bed. People learn to pray in different ways.

How did you learn to pray?

Prayer is a two-way communion. It's you talking to God, and then you pause and listen to what God says.

I want to give you several methods to see there is no right way or wrong way to pray and commune with God.

You will find many "how to pray" methods. You won't go lacking when you search for them.

There are many great methods and books on prayer available. There are many ways God uses to teach us how to pray. But let me tell you about an unconventional way that Eloise learned how to pray.

Eloise wanted to learn to pray. She was a new believer and prayer seemed formidable to her. She kept saying to her spiritual mom, Miss Shirley, that she didn't understand prayer or how to pray. Eloise would say it seemed weird to talk to a being she didn't know. She wanted to know how to approach such a person. "He is such a big God who controls everything; surely my prayers don't matter," she would say.

Miss Shirley asked her to come over on a Sunday afternoon, and she would explain it to her. Eloise went to her home and walked inside as usual. She didn't need to ring the bell; she knew it was okay to walk right in. Miss Shirley didn't mind. They had that kind of relationship. Eloise found Miss Shirley sitting in her favorite chair, eyes closed and rocking slowly. She sat across from her on the sofa and waited. Eloise looked around the room and then down at her feet, tapping the floor, wondering when Miss Shirley would speak. Eloise knew she wasn't sleeping because she was rocking. She knew Miss Shirley had to sense her presence there. As she kept waiting for what seemed like forever, she wondered when their discussion would begin. Miss Shirley was supposed to teach her how to pray today. When would she teach her about prayer and what to say to this big God?

After some uncomfortable minutes of silence, Eloise realized that Miss Shirley seemed peaceful. It was like she was somewhere else. Miss Shirley didn't notice her presence. She didn't seem to see anything in the room. Eloise noted that Miss Shirley seemed to be in the presence of someone else. It finally dawned on Eloise that Miss Shirley was in the presence of God. She was still and silent, and this was the lesson. She was listening.

Miss Shirley didn't say a word and let Eloise learn from watching her that this was prayer. This was communing with God.

Eloise never forgot the lesson she learned about prayer that day from watching her spiritual mom sit in the presence of a being so big and powerful yet so personal and real—that communing with Him in silence was prayer. Nothing more was needed.

The methods you will see below are different examples of how to pray.

METHOD #1
Five Basics of Prayer

A lot of people get bogged down by the techniques of prayer. They feel if they don't do it right, God won't hear them. Again, there is no one right or wrong way to pray. There are only guides on how to pray.

The Bible is full of scripture that tells us to pray and where, how, when, and who we should pray for. Let's look at them.

1. Where to Pray

"But when you pray, go into your room, close the door and pray to your Father, who is unseen. Then your Father, who sees what is done in secret, will reward you." (Matthew 6:6)

This verse tells us that Jesus said to pray in a dedicated place. It doesn't necessarily have to be a closet, but it can be. It's mainly telling you that prayer happens in a private place away from others where you can focus on the Lord. It's an intimate time where only God sees and hears your prayers.

Do you have a private place to pray? If so, where?

"The prayer of a righteous man is powerful and effective."

JAMES 5:16

2. How to Pray

"Our Father in heaven, hallowed be your name. Your kingdom come, your will be done, on earth as it is in heaven. Give us this day our daily bread, and forgive us our debts, as we also have forgiven our debtors. And lead us not into temptation, but deliver us from evil." (Matthew 6:9–15)

This famous passage of scripture is the pattern of prayer that the Lord gave to the disciples. It is a model prayer for believers to pray called the Lord's Prayer.

The model for prayer that Jesus gave is an invitation to a way to pray and will help you have a great prayer life that will be full of confidence.

It contains...

- praise,
- submission to His will,
- petition for daily needs, and
- requests for forgiveness and protection.

3. When to Pray

When to pray is a question that people have varying opinions about. Some say that you must pray in the morning to start your day with prayer. Others say to pray in the evening. It's not as crucial for the timing of prayer as it is your heart's position of prayer. God is not looking at the time. He is looking at you coming to Him from the invitation He gives to you.

1 Thessalonians 5:17 says to "pray continually."

When do you usually do most of your praying?

Read and write out 1 Thessalonians 5:16–18.

4. Who Should Pray?

Who should pray? You should pray. The Sermon on the Mount says this three times. Prayer is for you. It is not a guessing game, and you need not wonder. God wants you to pray.

Jesus repeated at least three times in Matthew 6, "when you pray." He was not giving the listeners an option. He was encouraging them that when they would pray, things would happen. When you pray, something will happen.

5. Who Do You Pray for?

The Word of God tells us who we are to pray for. So, if you are in confusion about who you pray for besides yourself, you need not be.

You are to pray for your enemies, saints, and everyone else.

Read and write out Ephesians 6:18.

Read and write out Matthew 5:44.

Read and write out 1 Timothy 2:1–2.

List the people you are praying for.

Your prayer time doesn't need to be a boring or dry time you spend with God. There are creative aids you can use to help you remember specific methods of prayer.

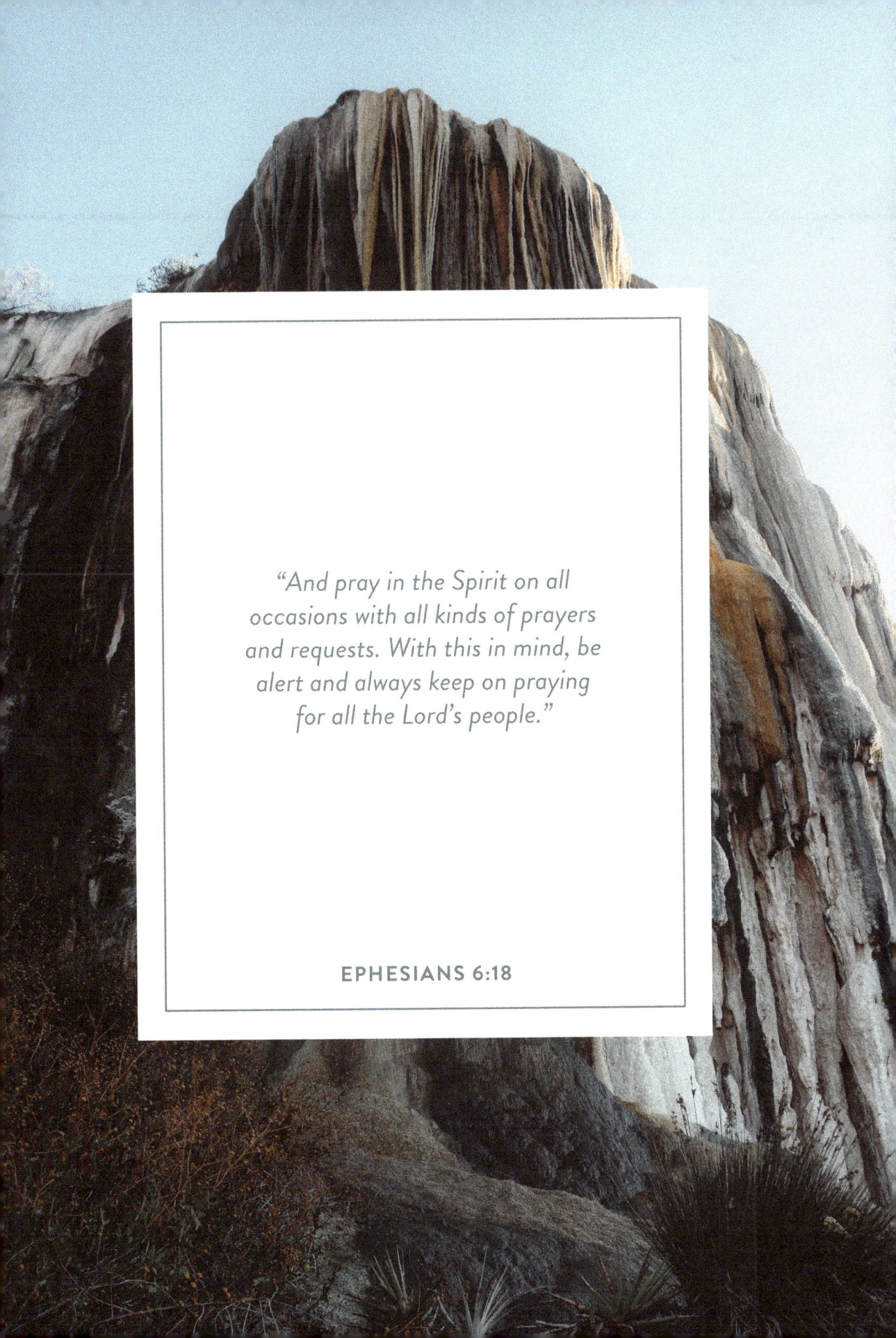

"And pray in the Spirit on all occasions with all kinds of prayers and requests. With this in mind, be alert and always keep on praying for all the Lord's people."

EPHESIANS 6:18

METHOD #2
Acronyms

There are several acronym prayers that you may have seen that can help you start and guide you in your prayer time. These are pretty easy to remember.

If you are a beginner in prayer and want to develop a solid prayer life, you may enjoy one of these.

- **T.S.P.**   Thanks, Sorry, Please
- **P.R.A.Y.**   Pray, Repent, Ask, Yield
- **P.U.S.H.**   Pray Until Something Happens
- **A.C.T.S.**   Adoration, Confession, Thanksgiving, Supplication

METHOD #3
The Five-Finger Prayer

This prayer involves using your hand and connecting your fingers to specific prayer points.

1. Your thumb is nearest to you. Begin by praying for those closest to you. They are the easiest people to remember. This can be a spouse, mother, father, children, etc.

2. The next finger is the pointing finger. Pray for those who teach, instruct, and heal. This may include teachers, doctors, ministers, instructors, etc. These individuals need support and wisdom as they point people in the right direction in life.

3. The next finger is the tallest. This finger reminds us of our leaders. It helps you to remember to pray for the head of state of your country, leaders in business and industry, government leaders and administrators, leaders of cities and states, and local leaders. These people help shape our nation, and they have a lot of pressure on them to be moral and upstanding. They need many prayers, and this is a great way to not forget them.

4. The fourth finger is the ring finger. This finger is the weakest and a reminder to pray for those who are the weakest in our society or those in trouble or pain. This could be the lost, the homeless, abandoned children, etc. They need much prayer and help from the Lord.

5. The last finger is the little finger. It is the smallest finger. This finger reminds you that the least shall be the greatest scripture, so pray for yourself last. After you have finished praying for the other groups of people, pray for yourself.

METHOD #4
Four-Step Prayer

Step 1: Address God the Father.

Step 2: Thank God for His blessings to you.

Step 3: Ask the Father for blessings.

Step 4: Close the prayer.

Let's look at these four steps a little closer if you are a beginner in prayer.

Step 1: Address God the Father

When you begin to pray, you can open your prayer by addressing God because He is the one you are praying to. Start by saying "Father in Heaven" or "Heavenly Father."

You address Him as your Heavenly Father because He is the Father of your soul. He is your creator and the one to whom you owe everything you have, including your life. He is the all-knowing and true God.

Step 2: Thank God for His blessings to You

After opening the prayer, tell your Father in Heaven what you are thankful for. Thank Him for all you have and all He has done for you. You can start by saying, "I thank you for..." or "I am grateful for..." You show your gratitude to your Heavenly Father by thanking Him in your prayer for your home, family, health, the earth, and other blessings of life.

Be sure to include general blessings such as safety and guidance and specific needs like divine protection while traveling.

Step 3: Ask the Father for blessings

After thanking your Father in Heaven, you can ask Him for help. Some of the ways you can do this are to say:

- "I ask you for..."

- "I need..."

- "Please help me, Father, with..."

You can ask God to bless you with things you need in life to help you bless another person. You can ask for knowledge, comfort, guidance, peace, direction, wisdom, etc.

Remember, God wants to answer you. He wants to bless you.

Step 4: Close or finish the prayer

You usually end your prayer by saying, "In the name of Jesus Christ, Amen." We do this because Jesus is our Savior, our mediator between death (physical and spiritual) and eternal life. We also say Amen because it means we accept or agree with what's been said.

Write out a practice prayer. Make it personal from your heart. Start your prayer with "Dear heavenly Father..."

"True, whole prayer is nothing but love."

– ST. AUGUSTINE

"But I tell you, love your enemies and pray for those who persecute you"

MATTHEW 5:44

Does Prayer Really Work?

An important question you may ask at some point in your life is, "Does prayer work?"

My sincere answer to you is YES! Prayer works.

At the beginning of your Christian walk, you may have noticed that almost anything you brought before the Lord was answered quickly.

Then as you progressed in your Christian walk, things didn't seem to get answered so quickly. Sometimes, because of this delay, you may have felt discouraged and asked, "Does prayer work for me?"

There are times when the discipline of prayer can be misunderstood because of the delay in response. We start to feel that prayer is work, and our words don't flow easily.

Sometimes, this delay can cause a person to give up the practice of prayer in their daily lives. I don't want that to be you.

Have you ever been frustrated with your praying? If so, describe why.

Does God hear me when I pray? Why are my prayers not answered? Why do I find praying tedious? Can my prayer be answered? Am I doing something to keep God from answering me?

These are all questions we sometimes wonder about in our prayer life.

Unanswered prayer is one of the main reasons many people don't pray like they should or engage in prayer very often.

Do you believe that you get answers to your prayers?

Let me share a story about how God answered a little boy's prayer. Let this story give you hope that God hears your prayers, and that prayer does work.

I want you to meet Joshua. Joshua and his mother Susan had almost nothing. They lived in the back of a house down a dark country road. Joshua was only eight years old but had suffered more than almost any other child. He had several health conditions, not to mention learning difficulties. When you met Joshua, all you noticed was how dirty his clothes were and how almost the entire top row of his teeth was rotted out. It was Christmas when Barbara and

Daniel met Joshua and his mom. Barbara and Daniel were looking for someone in need to help. The county had given them a name, and off they went.

Susan had fallen on difficult times and could only afford to stay in the back part of her uncle's abandoned home. This home had no heat and no furnishings to make it a home. It was unlivable. It was a rat trap. Barbara and Daniel went home and were completely heartbroken at the site and Joshua's condition.

As Barbara and Daniel talked to the mother and son, Barbara began to feel pain in her soul for the little boy. His eyes were filled with joy and hope even though his surroundings screamed something different. She asked him what he wanted for Christmas, knowing she could not offer much. Her heart was broken for this little boy standing before her. Joshua stated that he was hungry. He wanted food.

Barbara and Daniel told their two new friends that they would be back with food. As they drove off, they both knew what they had to do. They knew they were an answer to prayer for this tiny little family.

When they returned home, they gathered friends who could also help. Many people contributed. On Christmas Day, they visited Joshua and Susan with an entire community who helped furnish and repair their home, and who brought clothes, shoes, a Christmas tree, and a whole Christmas dinner along with more presents than they could have ever hoped for. Joshua and Susan were speechless.

Years later, Barbara found that same little boy on social media. As they were catching up, he told her the day that she and her husband Daniel came to their house was the day he knew God was real. "How?" she asked. He answered: "Because that was the day I asked God, 'If you are real, please bring me Christmas.'"

Prayer does work. It worked for a little boy, and it will work for you.

God is indeed a faithful God to answer prayer.

Why do you think many either don't pray or believe they will not get an answer to prayer?

*"Father, I thank you that
you have heard me. I knew that
you always hear me."*

JOHN 11:41-42

When you are starting to develop your prayer life, you may wonder how long you should pray, whether you should ask for what you want, and what you should ask for in prayer. These are normal questions.

This may be where you are right now. If so, believe in God and in your faith in God. God will show you how to grow in prayer.

As you accept your invitation to pray with God, these few things will help.

When these times come, try NOT to. . .

1. Feel abandoned by God.
2. Jump to conclusions about yourself and the prayer you prayed.
3. Question the character or integrity of God.
4. Feel that you cannot depend on God and begin to rely on yourself in life.

People usually go to these four things when they feel their prayer is not being answered. I want to encourage you that God will not abandon you.

His love for you and His invitation to prayer is about communion with you, His child. Try not to question the integrity of His character in those seasons of doubt. God is who He says He is.

What thoughts have you had about unanswered prayer in your own life?

Remember, prayer is not a duty, obligation, or activity like working a job. It is communion and heartfelt communication with God that touches His heart.

Prayer is not about begging God or arguing your case like a pauper. It is at the heart of a deep relationship with Him.

You begin at your level, and as you understand the foundations and principles of prayer, you start to communicate with Him with confidence.

Have you ever felt that God may have abandoned you in your prayer life?

Prayer is one of the most exciting and thrilling experiences you can have with God and your faith. Much happens in prayer that you cannot fathom.

Prayer transforms lives, changes circumstances, gives peace, and helps people to persevere in the world. Prayer can change the path of nations and the lives and careers of people every day.

Your prayers help bring people to the saving knowledge of Christ. They give hope to the hopeless, like Joshua.

Describe a time you knew that your prayer changed someone for whom you were praying.

Your prayers are critical.

Let's look at some more scripture about God answering prayers to build your confidence.

Read and write out 1 John 5:14-15.

This verse is special in that the Lord gives us great certainty that He hears and answers our prayer so much that He wants us to believe it before it happens.

God wants you to believe that your prayers will be answered. Prayer creates intimacy with God, causing you to trust Him more and His love, and bringing honor to His nature and character.

God desires that you pray with understanding and pray with power.

Think about this. Prayer is meant to be answered, or God would not ask you to pray and pray without ceasing, never giving up.

Jesus knew that God always answered Him and heard Him.

John 11:41–42 says, *"Father, I thank you that you have heard me. I knew that you always hear me."*

How would an answer to a prayer affect your life right now?

Remember, prayer is NOT about getting God to do what you desire, but about knowing Him, being in a relationship with Him to know His will, and doing His will.

Prayer reminds you that you are not in control, but God is in control. It helps keep you close to Him and His heart.

"I pray because I can't help myself. ... I pray because the need flows out of me all the time, waking and sleeping. It doesn't change God. It changes me."

– C.S. LEWIS

"And we know that in all things God works for the good of those who love him, who have been called according to his purpose"

ROMANS 8:28

Hindrances to Prayer

We have looked at what prayer is, how to pray, why it is important, and whether it works.

In this session, we will look at the hindrances to prayer. I know we don't like them, but according to the Bible there are things that hinder prayer.

Before we begin, I want to ask you a question.

What do you think hinders your prayer?

Let's look at what the Bible says are the reasons prayer is hindered.

NOT ASKING ACCORDING TO THE SCRIPTURES OR THE WILL OF GOD.

Read and write out 1 John 5:14–15.

God is clear about you asking according to His will. The wonderful scripture above should give you confidence in asking and knowing He heard you.

Read and write out Matthew 6:10.

This verse is a portion of the Lord's prayer. The will of God on earth is the same as the will of God in heaven. You can be assured that God will hear and answer your prayer according to these promises.

When you get discouraged because an answer seems not to be coming, go back to these anchor promises.

Meditating on scripture is key to knowing the promises of God for your life when discouragement and uncertainty come. Let's look at a few more hindrances.

Not Praying in Faith

Read and write out Mark 11:24.

Whatever you pray, God wants you to pray and believe it. Don't disbelieve it. Have a deep resolve that He will answer your request. He is a God who wants you to take Him at His word. Don't doubt when you ask Him anything.

Read and write out James 1:6.

Not Being Obedient

Disobedience is probably the most significant hindrance. The Lord loves obedience. It is the key to your walk with God. Learn to obey God even if it costs you. Don't compromise things in your life so that your confidence in asking is weakened. Be obedient at all costs in your personal life and spiritual life.

Read and write out Psalms 66:18.

Remember, you have learned that prayer is a relationship with God. When sin or anything else hinders this relationship or displeases the Lord, it will be hard for your prayer to be answered.

God delights in an upright heart.

Read and write out Proverbs 15:8.

Read and write out Proverbs 15:29.

Sometimes there will be unanswered prayers for reasons we don't understand or may never know.

Unanswered prayer happens because God doesn't always reveal His complete will to us about situations and circumstances. We must learn to trust that His way is perfect and that He is good, no matter what occurs.

Continue to trust God and believe that all things work together for good and that things will work out as they should in the end. God will never reject you or leave you. His promises are true for you even if your prayer appears to go unanswered.

Read and write out Romans 8:28.

Not Confessing Sins

In this life, you will not live a flawlessly sinless life. That is not a requirement of answered prayer. God knows this. That is why you need Jesus and need His blood to cleanse you from sin. But confession of sin is essential for God to forgive your sins. Always take the time in prayer to confess any sin and be cleansed by the sacrifice of Jesus' blood.

Read and write out 1 John 1:9.

Obedience to Him in your life is crucial, but it is never perfect as long as we live, so confession must be made. God is faithful and just, and He will forgive you.

Read and write out 1 John 3:21–22.

Not Forgiving Others

A great hindrance to prayer is unforgiveness. Forgiveness is at the heart of the Bible. The Lord's prayer clearly states that you will not be forgiven unless you forgive. We ask God to forgive our sins according to the same standard we have used in forgiving the sins of others.

When you don't forgive, your sins are not forgiven.

Read and write out Matthew 6:14–15.

Sin separates us from God, and forgiveness of that sin restores it. Until that happens, it can be difficult to pray until we forgive others.

Take some time to look at these areas of hindrance and see if you need to address anything in your personal life.

"But when you ask, you must believe and not doubt, because the one who doubts is like a wave of the sea, blown and tossed by the wind."

– JAMES 1:6

"your kingdom come,
your will be done,
on earth as it is in heaven"

MATTHEW 6:10

The Ultimate Conversation

As this study comes to an end, if you would like to pray a prayer of salvation or rededicate your life to God, I welcome you to do that now. You may read this study and realize that you want to begin a new relationship with God. You may desire a stronger relationship with Him through prayer and need to rededicate your life.

Here is a prayer that you can pray to do just that.

Dear Heavenly Father,

Today I rededicate my life to You. I want to receive you as my Lord and Savior. I believe that Jesus is your Son and that You raised Him from the dead. I believe this with all my heart. I commit my heart, my mind, my words, my actions, everything I have, and everything I am to You. I purposely draw close to You, and I thank You that You draw near to me. I repent of all known sins in my life and ask that You forgive me of any unrepented sin. Likewise, I forgive anyone that has sinned against me. I set them free and let the offenses go. I now receive Your love, Your instruction, comfort, and guidance. Thank You for welcoming me and for this new fresh start and new life with You.

In Jesus' Name, Amen.

WAYS TO
CONNECT

For more information, please visit Ruth's website, www.ruthhovsepian.com, where you will find her podcast, blog, videos, speaking calendar, free resources, and all her latest news and information.

To book Ruth to speak at your next event, please visit ruthhovsepian.com or email info@ruthhovsepian.com for more details.

www.ingramcontent.com/pod-product-compliance
Lightning Source LLC
Chambersburg PA
CBHW041540120626
46551CB00019B/2774